Animals
in the Sun

by Donna Foley

PEARSON

Scott
Foresman

Editorial Offices: Glenview, Illinois • Parsippany, New Jersey • New York, New York
Sales Offices: Needham, Massachusetts • Duluth, Georgia • Glenview, Illinois
Coppell, Texas • Sacramento, California • Mesa, Arizona

ISBN: 0-328-13157-1

Many hot animals
make their homes here.

Many hot animals
have fun in the sun.

Many hot hippos
go into a pond.

Many hot elephants
go into a pond.

Many hot zebras
go into a pond.

A pond is the best spot for them.